STORIES THAT STRENGTHEN

STORIES THAT STRENGTHEN

Compiled by Lucy Gertsch Thomson

BOOKCRAFT, INC.
Salt Lake City, Utah

Library of Congress Catalog Card Number: 75-15083
ISBN 0-88494-281-3

1st Printing, 1975

LITHOGRAPHED IN U.S.A. BY
PUBLISHERS PRESS
SALT LAKE CITY, UTAH

Contents

Adversity

What Is God Trying to Teach Me Now?

Linda wanted to be a cheerleader. She wanted this more than anything she had ever wanted before. Every spare minute she had away from her school work was spent in practicing cheerleading drills and routines.

At night when Linda closed her eyes for sleep she could picture herself in front of stands filled with shouting people. Bands were playing, people were laughing, excitement was in the air. She would be dressed in her beautiful uniform with its glittering sequins and would lead the cheering crowd in thunderous yells that would inspire the team to victory! The boys on the team would notice her too and after the game she would need to decide which date to accept to the victory dance.

However, it was a different Linda that left the cheerleading tryouts. She had done a really fine job, the judges told her, but other girls were better.

To keep from brooding over this failure, Linda began playing the piano again. She had almost forgotten how. Cheerleading had left her little if any time for piano practice.

Now, with added practice, her piano skill was returning. Linda was asked more and more often to play the piano in church, at parties, and at school. She began singing too. Her clear, sweet voice brought happiness to all who listened. Her teachers and friends were very pleased and encouraged her to try even harder. Linda was popular and was respected by a wide circle of friends.

One night after a very nice musical program Linda was heard to say, "I felt very sorry for myself when I was not chosen as a cheerleader. I thought my whole world was ended. Now I realize it was a blessing. It would have been fun to be a cheerleader, but my special talent is music. If I had continued to spend my time in cheerleading, I may never have resumed my music lessons. I've learned that when things seem to go wrong for us, we should look for the brighter side. We should ask ourselves the question, 'What is God trying to teach me now?' "

— Wayne B. Lynn.

Atonement

Of Foolish Ventures

Something was wrong with my dog Spotty. I could tell by the way he was acting. Instead of his usual bounding, barking, tail-wagging greeting, he slipped like a shadow around the corner of the building.

Sensing his need for my attention, I, too, slipped around the building to learn the reason for his strange behavior. A quick glance was all that was needed to tell the story. Spotty's face was bristling with white-pointed slivers that gave him the look of a grizzled old prospector whose face was covered with whiskers. He whimpered pleadingly and rubbed his nose toward the ground and pawed at his face and lips trying to remove the cause of his pain. A porcupine had driven a multitude of sharp quills deep into his tender nose and quivering flesh.

He saw me now and looked up toward me with pleading eyes as if to say, "I know I have been foolish. I should have known better, but won't you please help me?" He made another futile pass at the cruel barbs protruding from his bloodied face which merely added to his pain and further proved the hopelessness of his situation.

I walked over to my nearby car, removed a pair of pliers from the glove compartment, and walked back toward him. "This is going to hurt, old fella," I said softly as I carefully pillowed his pain-ridden head in my lap. He looked back at me with limpid eyes as if to say, "I understand."

As I began making the painful extractions, I talked to him quietly. I suppose I was talking to myself as much as I was to him. "What would you do without me now, old fella? You are in a rather hopeless situation, aren't you? How would you ever get these quills out by yourself?" He looked directly at me, and I felt he understood. I wondered what would have happened to him if I had not come to his aid. I could imagine those painful barbs finding their way deeper and deeper into fevered flesh, his face festering and swelling as the pain became so unrelenting that he would do most anything to escape from it.

"How like old Spotty we are," I thought to myself. "How many times do we find ourselves in foolish circumstances from which we cannot escape?"

My thoughts carried me to a man kneeling in a garden alone. Upon him was placed the burden of all the sins of the world. The weight of this debt brought pain and anguish beyond our understanding, pain of such magnitude that he, the Son of God, sweat blood from every pore.

I thought of my own life, of foolish ventures that brought me sorrow; but because of him who knelt alone in the garden, I could be spared. Jesus had done that for me which I could not do for myself. My pain could be removed, my tortured spirit healed. I could look up once again with hope and promise.

I could feel old Spotty tremble with pain each time I touched him, but he made no protest. Finally, the last quill was removed from his sad face. I stroked his fevered head gently and felt the warm softness of his fur beneath my finger-tips. With a painful effort he lifted his head and turned with gratitude to lick my hand.

My thoughts returned to Jesus. His feet were bathed in tears and dried with the hair of a repentant sinner. I longed to show my love to him, to bathe his feet with my tears, to kneel before him.

Spotty was all right now. He rose stiffly and walked cautiously away with his tail scribing small arcs of happiness. We had learned something today, Spotty and I, something for which I am grateful.

— Wayne B. Lynn.

Attitude

You Needn't Have Everything to Be Happy

In 1951, I became totally blind from an acute attack of glaucoma. I cried while I was in the hospital, but this only made my eyes hurt and didn't help anything. As I thought of my six children, I decided I would never let my blindness hurt them, and I would learn to do everything. I decided to accept my blindness as a challenge, since everyone has problems, and no one has everything.

It was Saturday morning when I came home from the hospital. The first thing I tried to do was to scrub the kitchen floor. I scrubbed an area and when it felt smooth to my hand, I went on to the next area. There were piles of washing awaiting me. I found that my hands could easily tell the difference between towels, sheets, stockings and shirts. When I had finished washing a load, I piled the damp pieces on my shoulder and walked out into the backyard with my right hand up in the air until I contacted the clothesline. It was easy to hang the clothes on the line.

Vacuuming is the most difficult household task, because I have to go over the whole carpet with my hands to be sure nothing is on the floor that will cause trouble in the vacuum. When I wash dishes, I have to "see" every part of every dish, glass, kettle, knife, fork and spoon with my hands to check them as I rinse them with hot water. When I cook vegetables, I place the kettle on the ring, and then turn on the heat so I don't burn my hands centering the kettle on the ring. When I bake bread, I tap the bread. If it sounds hollow, I know it is done. Cookies can be tested by taking one out and tasting it.

I learned braille, and could braille all of my packages and cans, but if the shape, weight, size and aroma didn't identify the food before I opened it, I just preferred to be surprised.

Until I became blind I never thanked my Heavenly Father for my hands, but now I thank him all day long. As I fix my bed in the morning, I feel the evenness of the sheets and covers on one side, then finish the other side and smooth the top of the bed. When I bring in the mail, the different envelopes tell me that some are commercial, some are personal, and some are advertising. Of course I must wait until someone who is sighted comes along to read the mail. I learned to type fifty years ago and have no difficulty sending out my correspondence. Do you know that these marvelous hands are the pattern for almost all of the mechanical inventions? Hands do a million intricate jobs, yet we rarely stop to appreciate their genius.

I never thanked Heavenly Father for my eyes until after I became blind. Now I have a keen awareness of the intelligence that could create the human eye. We have a curved windshield (cornea) and every three seconds the eyelid, using a drop of antiseptic fluid from the tear gland, washes this beautiful window. Underneath the cornea is the lens that can make a hundred different adjustments to give clear sight. The colored part of the eye, the iris, is an automatic light adjustment meter. At the back of the eye is the retina, as thin as a razor blade, which has rods and cones that make it possible for us to see in color and in three dimensions.

A million nerve responses per second carry sight pictures to the brain for interpretation and filing. I am grateful for the brain file, because I can recall beautiful drives through the canyon, and remember how people and myriad things were when I could see. Especially am I grateful for color. If I touch a rose, and someone tells me what color it is, I can visualize it and enjoy its beauty along with the velvet of its petals, its form and its fragrance.

I appreciate the exquisite design of fruits and vegetables. When I cut an apple in half crosswise, I can still visualize the star design which has a little package for each seed. Each seed has the potential of creating an apple tree. We applaud man-made plastic coverings, but the skin of the apple is not only beautiful, it preserves the food value and eating quality of the apple for months.

Blindness, although inconvenient, has been interesting. It is a constant challenge to invent ways of doing what needs to be done or what I want to do. Fortunately, I was able to keep on teaching piano, but because I could not read new music, I had to learn new music by listening to it, and I also decided to compose music. I wrote a little song, "Pioneer Children Sang as They Walked and Walked," because I know we are all pioneers every day and either we can sing as we walk through the day or we can grouch every step of the way. When the Primary published this song, I was encouraged to write many other children's songs. I wrote "Book of Mormon Stories" because I am so grateful for America and because I know we were "given this land if we'll live righteously." I now have a group of about a hundred of my compositions. I probably never would have composed music if I had been sighted because there are millions of great compositions available on the market today.

In the New Testament we read that the people brought a blind man to the Savior and asked him who had sinned, this man or his parents, that he was born blind. The Savior replied that neither this man nor his parents had sinned, but that he was born blind to show the glory of God.

It has been said that in the beginning everything can seem impossible to us. In 1951, I would not have believed that all the living and working and problem-solving that has given me so much pleasure could have been accomplished. I feel that it is a great sin to be unhappy. We can always be happy if we develop our appreciation and gratitude, and remember that problems are only opportunities and that joy will come to those who work through every day and endure to the end.

— Elizabeth Fetzer Bates.

Courage

Sergeant Stewart

I met him just once — at a sacrament meeting held with the LDS servicemen of the 15th Regiment, 3rd Infantry Division, during the Korean War. There were about fifteen of us crowded into a front-line bunker. Using our own canteen cups and C-ration crackers, we blessed and partook of the sacrament; and since it was the first Sunday of the month we then turned the time over to the bearing of testimonies.

He introduced himself simply as Sergeant Stewart from Idaho, and proceeded to tell us how the Lord had blessed him during the previous month. I noted that he was short — about 5'5" tall — and weighed about 160 pounds, with strong arms and shoulders. He mentioned that his great ambition since childhood had been to become a good athlete. Coaches had considered him small for team sports, so he had concentrated on individual competition and had gained some success as a wrestler and distance runner. He had arrived in Korea with the rank of private. Some ten months later he was wearing sergeant's stripes — and they were well-deserved, as we would soon discover.

As he bore his testimony, Sergeant Stewart was moved to tell us about his company commander, whom he described as a giant of a man named Lieutenant Jackson. He was 6'7" tall, weighed a hulking 245 pounds, and had been an outstanding college athlete. The sergeant spoke of him in glowing, somewhat biased terms, as the bravest, sharpest, and greatest company commander in the entire U.S. Infantry — one who would not ask his men to do anything he would not first be willing to do himself. With noticeable pride he further depicted him as a man's man, a tremendous officer, and a Christian gentleman, inspiring those who were fortunate enough to serve under his command.

A few days prior to our church service Sergeant Stewart had been assigned to a patrol. Leading and at the point of the patrol was Lieutenant Jackson. Bringing up the rear, as they moved down the steep hill in diamond formation, was the sergeant. As they neared the base of the hill, they were ambushed by enemy snipers. The Lieutenant, being out in front, was riddled up one side by automatic small-arms fire. As he fell he managed to drag himself to the shelter of a nearby rock and tree, while the rest of the patrol scrambled up the hill to regroup.

Since he was next in command, the responsibility of the patrol now fell upon the shoulders of Sergeant Stewart. He immediately formed his men into a "half-moon" perimeter defense and then assigned his largest and seemingly strongest man the mission of going down the hill to rescue the Lieutenant. The others would provide him with cover.

The man was gone for approximately half an hour, only to return and report that he could not budge the wounded officer — he was too heavy. It was like trying to lift a dead horse. The men started grumbling about getting out of there before someone else got hit. Someone was heard to say, "Let's forget about the Lieutenant. . . ." At this point Sergeant Stewart turned to his men, and pulling himself up to his full sixty-five-inch stature he spoke in very matter-of-fact tones: "We're not leaving without him. He wouldn't leave any of us in similar circumstances. Besides, he's our commanding officer and I love him like my own brother."

There was a moment of silence, and then the sergeant approached one of the corporals and said quietly but with great authority. "You take charge — and wait for us. I will bring him back."

Carefully, and as noiselessly as possible, he inched his way among sporadic sniper fire toward the Lieutenant. When he finally reached him, Lieutenant Jackson was weak from loss of blood, and he assured the sergeant that it was a hopeless cause — there would be no way to get him back to the aid station in time. It was then that Sergeant Stewart's great faith in his Heavenly Father came to his assistance. He took off his helmet, knelt beside his fallen leader and said, "Pray with me, Lieutenant."

We were held spellbound in that meeting. It was as though we were witnessing one of the great human dramas of our day. A spiritual drama of love and brotherhood, so lacking in today's world, was unfolding before our very eyes. Tears rolled down the Sergeant's cheeks as he spoke — and we wept silently with him. He couldn't remember all he had said in his prayer, but he recalled reminding the Lord that never in his life had he smoked a cigarette. Not once had he tasted alcohol in any of its forms.

At this point he digressed for a moment to explain that he had abstained from liquor and tobacco not only because it was his religious belief, but also because of his great motivation to develop a strong, healthy body in order to achieve his athletic aspirations. That day, however, as he communed with his Father in heaven, he knew without doubt why he had lived the Word of Wisdom so conscientiously throughout his young life.

"Dear Lord," he pleaded, "I need strength — far beyond the capacity of my physical body. This great man, thy son, who lies critically wounded here beside me, must have medical attention soon. I need the power to carry him up this hill to an aid station where he can receive the treatment he needs to preserve his life. I know, Father, that thou hast promised the strength of ten to him whose heart and hands are clean and pure. *I feel I can qualify.* Please, Dear Lord, grant me this blessing."

"Brethen," he continued, "as I prayed I could feel my muscles bulge with energy and I knew at that moment, as I had never known before, that God truly hears and answers the prayers of his faithful children. I humbly thanked him, said amen, put on my helmet, reached down and gently picked up my company commander and cradled him over my shoulder. We then started slowly our ascent up the hill — Lieutenant Jackson crying softly as he whispered to me words of gratitude and encouragement."

I met Sergeant Stewart just once. For less than two hours it was our privilege to be in his company. I could feel the presence of greatness as I sat in that bunker listening to that choice young man. His spirit touched my spirit, and my faith was kindled because of his Christlike attitude and his soul-stirring testimony regarding the fatherhood of God and the brotherhood of all men.

— Ben F. Mortensen, *Instructor,* March 1969, pp. 82-83.

Creativity

Silent Night

A little hole eaten in the bellows of an organ in a village near Salzburg, Austria, prompted the beautiful song, "Silent Night." Because of a raging storm, no one could come high up in the mountains to fix the hole in the organ that Christmas Eve in the year eighteen hundred and eighteen.

As the priest sat alone in his study, wondering how services could be held without an organ, he was impressed with the deep, penetrating quietness, and how humble man really was after all — that a hungry little mouse could leave them almost helpless to properly conduct their most important Christmas Eve services. It must have been humble and quiet in the manger that night long ago, he thought to himself.

He listened, and there was only silence. Silent night — yes, and it was a holy night. All is calm, all is bright. Then he wrote — "Round yon virgin mother and child. Holy infant, so tender and mild." Rapidly his pen flew across the parchment, recording his thoughts.

Franz Gruber, his good friend, made a tune for the words, and the priest, Josef Mohr, rejoiced when his parishioners sang this new song without organ music.

— Author unidentified.

An Idea

Eli Whitney conceived the idea of the cotton gin when he saw a cat which had killed a chicken try to pull the chicken through a fence. The space was too narrow. Every time the cat's claw came out, it held nothing but feathers. He resolved to build an iron claw which would pull the cotton through a fine mesh, leaving the seeds behind. Only a week later Eli Whitney had completed a rough draft of his cotton gin.

— Author unidentified.

Divine Help

A Voice Told Her What to Do

[The remote little town of Bluff was without a doctor. Sister Haskell, who had acted as midwife, had moved to San Luis Valley. Bishop Jens Nielson and his counselors canvassed the area as they had done before, in search of a doctor. They decided upon young Jody Wood.]

It was not because of any medical training which she had received that they decided on her — her schooling had been in an old-time, primitive school, under many difficulties. Like the call the Church makes to its thousands of missionaries, not because they are already qualified but because they will qualify for the work by beginning to do it, her call was to be a doctor by the same inspiration which makes the farmer, the truck driver, the carpenter into a missionary.

The prospect was terrifying; she protested that she knew nothing about medicine, was utterly unfit for the work, and could not do it and still care for her little children. The brethren told her she *could* do it, that they would place their hands on her head and bless her for that mission, and that she would be given understanding.

Deep in the soul of Josephine Chatterly Wood was something solid and dependable — a revealed testimony of the gospel. It taught her that all the calls which the Lord makes through his duly authorized servants must be obeyed. This was the way of the Lord in his Church, and his people in obedience to it are provided for in time of need. She understood this clearly, and in spite of her fears, and the great labors the mission would place upon her, she accepted it in humility and tears.

Although Aunt Jody knew little of books and literature, she had been highly educated in the university of the frontier, being fitted with practical skill and adaptability which she could have acquired in no other way. Hers was the unusual ability to find a way or to make a way through or over or around every and all difficulties. Her faith and her resourcefulness counted for more than any university degree she might have held. The part she took, and the way she carried on with it until she died under the weight of it, is possible only to people who believe in God and who believe in themselves as his servants.

We quote her daughter, Mrs. Catherine Hansen, whose words we may use frequently in this account: "When the first call came for a confinement case, Mother was afraid. My father blessed her, asking the Lord to guide her and give her wisdom for any emergency she might have to meet. In this he was setting a precedent for many occasions of the future. Ofttimes the whole family knelt in prayer for Mother as she went forth on her mission of mercy."

Bishop Nielson had promised Aunt Jody that if she would do her best, she would be directed by the Holy Spirit. She had assured him she would do all she could, and she had purchased books and studied and prayed. Yet, faced with the stern reality of being responsible where life and death hung in the balance, something she had never faced before, she asked the bishop to go with her. And she did meet the emergency for which Brother Wood had prayed she might have the necessary wisdom: "The cord was wrapped around the baby's neck, and someone spoke to her telling her what to do. She removed the cord and saved the little one's life. Speaking of it later, she said, 'I thought Bishop Nielson had spoken to me, but when I turned to look at him, he was not in the room. I knew the Lord had blessed me, telling me plainly what to do.' "

— Excerpt from Albert R. Lyman, "Aunt Jody, Nurse of the San Juan Frontier," *Improvement Era,* September 1958.

A Voice of Warning

James England, the first bishop of Union Stake, Union County, Oregon, tells this incident.

As a young man, he obtained employment in the Colorado mines. One day while working in the mine he thought he heard his mother call his name, although she was many miles away from Colorado. Twice he heard the call, "Jim!" The voice was so distinct that he went outside the mine to see if she had come to see him. Just as he came out of the mine, it caved in. His life was saved by being obedient to the voice of warning.

— Author unidentified.

How the Oxen Were Found

When President Joseph F. Smith was a boy nine years old a remarkable thing happened to him and his mother.

His mother, who was a widow, and his uncle and Joseph were on their way home from St. Joseph, Missouri. Their home was just then at Winter Quarters, near what is now Florence, Nebraska. It was just after the Saints had been driven from Illinois and before they came to Utah. Joseph, his mother and his uncle, had been to St. Joseph to get provisions for the family.

On their journey home they camped one evening at the edge of a small prairie, or open flat, surrounded by woods. There was a large herd of cattle on their way to market being pastured nearby for the night. Mrs. Smith's little company of three turned out their teams as usual to graze. In the morning their best yoke of oxen was missing. They were greatly surprised at this, because the animals had never before separated from the rest. Joseph and his uncle at once started in search of them, over the prairie through the tall, wet grass into the woods. They searched and searched till they were tired and hungry and their legs wet to the skin, but without finding the oxen.

Joseph got back to the wagons first. It was towards noon. As he approached the wagons he saw that his mother was praying. Pretty soon his uncle came. As they had had nothing to eat since the night before, Sister Smith said:

"Now, you two had better eat your breakfast, and while you are doing so, I'll go and see if I can find the oxen."

The two looked at her surprised.

"It's perfectly useless for you to go out for the oxen," said the uncle. "Joseph and I have been out all morning, and I have inquired of the herdsmen and everybody I've met. I believe they have been driven off."

Joseph was somewhat of the same opinion. Still his mother had been praying, and if anybody could find them she could, he believed. He had never known his mother to pray without getting what she had prayed for, because she was a woman of great faith. And when his mother had gone and his uncle was attending to the other animals, he knelt down and prayed that she would find them, and exercised all the faith in her behalf that he could muster.

Sister Smith went straight for a thicket of willows on the little stream where they were camped. As she approached it one of the men who were herding the cattle that were on their way to the market, said to her:

"Madam, I saw your oxen this morning over in the woods," pointing in the direction away from where she was going.

She paid no attention to him whatever, but went on straight for the willows.

"I say, your cattle are not that way!" he shouted. "They're over there!" and he pointed the same way he had pointed before.

She said not a word but passed on.

Then the man rode as fast as his horse could carry him, and soon he was with his companions following the herd to St. Joseph.

Mrs. Smith went on till she got to the bushes toward which she had been going all along. In the dense cluster of these willows she found her oxen so entangled in the brush and tied up by means of willows that had been fastened round their necks, that she had great difficulty in getting them untied. This herder who had run away to his companions had tried to steal them, had tied them up as fast as he could, and then tried to turn Mrs. Smith away from them so that she would not find them.

— *Children's Friend.*

Fed by Quail in Modern Days

[The Missouri mob expelled the last remnant of Mormons from Nauvoo in September of 1846. The group numbered about six hundred and forty. This group was comprised of those who were either too poor to purchase an outfit with which to leave the city, or else those who could not dispose of their property to buy teams with which to remove.

When driven from their homes by the mob they took refuge on the Iowa side of the Mississippi river, where they bivouacked as best they could on the river bottoms. Colonel Kane visited this encampment and describes the conditions, saying:]

"Dreadful indeed, was the suffering of these forsaken beings; bowed and cramped by cold and sunburn, alternating as each weary day and night dragged on, they were, almost all of them, the crippled victims of disease. They were there because they had no homes, nor hospitals, nor poor house, nor friends to offer them any. They could not satisfy the feeble cravings of their sick; they had not bread to quiet the fractious hunger-cries of their children. Mothers and babes, daughters and grandparents, all of them alike, were bivouacked in tatters,

wanting even covering to comfort those whom the sick shivers
of fever were searching to the marrow."

[This] encampment was improvised of such materials as
were at hand. There were a few old wagons with covers:
tents were constructed by stretching quilts and blankets over
frames made of small poles; other shelters still were made
by weaving brush between stakes driven into the ground; and
here were huddled women and children destitute of both food
and adequate clothing. It was the latter part of September,
and the cold fall rains frequently drenched them. It was the
sickly season of the year and most of the camp suffered from
alternating chills and fever. Such as were able to leave camp
went into neighboring towns up and down the river and
applied to farmers and settlers about them for work and
relief from starvation. Their camp, from the general destitu-
tion that prevailed, is called in the Church annals, "the poor
camp." In the midst of their greatest distress for want of
food, a most remarkable circumstance, yet well attested, happened. This was no other than the falling into their camp —
and for several miles up and down the river — of immense
numbers of quail. The birds are quite common in that country,
but these flocks were so exhausted, evidently from a long flight,
that the women and children and even the sick, since they
came tumbling into the tent or bowers, could take them up
with their hands. Thousands were so caught, and the sick and
the destitute were fed upon daintiest food.

No sooner was the news of the results of the Battle of
Nauvoo carried to the headquarters of Brigham Young, on the
Missouri, and the destitute condition of the expelled saints
made known, than a relief company was organized consisting
of teams with tents and provisions to make the journey back
to the Mississippi, to gather up the victims of the mob's hate
and violence. This relief company started eastward under the
direction of O. M. Allen. In due time the saints of "the poor
camp" — as these helpless refugees were called — were brought
away from the scenes of their afflictions, and found refuge
among their friends in the camps on the Missouri.

The quail incident occurred upon the 9th of October and is thus recorded in the History of Brigham Young, Manuscript: "On the 9th of October, while our teams were waiting on the banks of the Mississippi for the poor saints . . . left without any of the necessaries of life, . . . and nothing to start their journey with, the Lord sent flocks of quail, which lit upon their wagons and their empty tables, and upon the ground within their reach, which the saints, and even the sick caught with their hands until they were satisfied." (Book 2, pp. 382-383). This phenomenon extended some 30 or 40 miles along the river, and was generally observed. The quail in immense quantities had attempted to cross the river, but it being beyond their strength, had dropped into the river boats or on the bank. (Wells, in Utah Notes, Ms., 7. *History of the Church*, Cannon, *Juvenile Instructor*, Vol. xviii, p. 107. Also letter of Brigham Young to Elders Hyde, Pratt and Taylor, of January 6th, 1847; *Millennial Star*, Vol. ix, p. 99).

— *Comprehensive History of the Church*, Vol. 3, pp. 135-136.

What Frightened Pancho Villa?

Villa had sworn vengeance on the United States and all Yankees wherever he found them and as he swept northward, murdered several US. citizens who fell into his hands.

On March 9, he and his band thundered into the border town of Columbus, New Mexico, killing, burning and looting.

The news of Villa's reign of terror flashed through the U.S. and Mexico. In Salt Lake City, Elder Anthony W. Ivins of the Council of the Twelve and former president of Juarez Stake in Mexico, went to the temple to fast and pray. He knew the terrible danger of the saints in Colonia Juarez and Colonia Dublan.

The people in the two towns were no less aware of the impending massacre and were desperately casting about for a means of escape.

Bishop Anson B. Call, his counselors, W. Ernest Young and Nephi Thayne, and the rest of the men of Dublan, gathered one afternoon in front of the Romney-Farnsworth Store. They knew that Villa had been twenty miles north in Corralitos for nearly three days; that he soon would come south to hide in the mountains because the U.S. Army was on his trail; that Dublan lay directly in his path and that he would slaughter the Mormons just as he had killed every other Yankee he had found.

There was much serious discussion about what should be done. Some were for hiding in the mountains. Others suggested going to Nueve Casas Grandes where there was a federal garrison.

After all the pros and cons had been aired, Bishop Call made the decision: "Everybody go home, turn off your lamps, pray and go to bed." The people followed his counsel.

In Corralitos, there was much activity. The Villa camp was getting ready to move. Maximiano and el Huero were busy far into the night packing equipment and supplies. At midnight, the guerrillas mounted their horses and headed south on the road to Dublan.

Three hours later, they reached the outskirts of the Mormon community. This would be more sport than Columbus, the men assured each other, as they looked greedily at the darkened houses.

Suddenly Villa signalled a halt. "Turn to the left!" he commanded. "Let's get out of here fast!"

"But why!" exclaimed his amazed lieutenants. "The town is ours for the taking."

"Fools, can't you see? The town is full of lights and soldiers!" Pancho almost shouted. "Vamonos — let's go!"

Maximiano and el Huero could hardly believe their ears. They and the rest of the troops saw no lights, no soldiers — just a ripe plum ready to be plucked.

Nevertheless, they followed their leader off to the southeast. Instead of spending the rest of the night in comfortable

Mormon homes, they rode nearly until dawn and slept on the stony ground at Chocolate Pass.

Next morning, the people came out and looked at the tracks of the horses that had veered away from the town and left them sleeping peacefully.

No one knew what had happened until some time later when Maximiano and el Huero left the Villa camp and told the story to one of the colonists.

— Arnold Irvine, *Church News,* March 2, 1968.

Drunkenness

He Drank the Wine

An Arab legend tells about the devil appearing to a man saying, "You are about to die. I can spare your life if you choose to do one of the following things: Kill your servant, beat your wife, or drink this wine." The man reflected a moment. It was unthinkable to harm his faithful servant, and ridiculous to mistreat his wife, so he drank the wine.

He drank the wine and, being drunk, beat his wife and killed his servant who attempted to defend her.

— Author unidentified.

Example

By Their Fruits

Alan Harris and Ed Hoppes had become acquainted in the service. Harris was a Mormon boy from Layton, Utah.

EXAMPLE   21

He was a medical technician. Hoppes was an X-ray technician from Springfield, Ohio.

Both struck it off very well. Neither cared for night spots. Whenever they had liberty, they went for long hikes and visited historical places. They sometimes just lay on the grass and watched the clouds. They didn't talk to each other a great deal except about farming. They discussed religion very little.

Alan didn't learn for many years that his actions and his clean living habits communicated more to Ed than the words they exchanged.

When the war with Japan was over, both servicemen returned to their respective homes. Ed Hoppes became a contractor and became involved in building homes. He was laying plans to develop the village of Northridge.

One day three young married women came to his office.

"We are known as Mormons," they said.

They had been authorized by the leaders of the branch to contact Mr. Hoppes to see if he would sell them a piece of land where they could build a chapel.

"I had a good friend in the service who was a member of your Church," he told the women. "I was inspired and impressed by the clean and wholesome life he led. I'll tell you what I'll do. I'll give you the ground you need upon which to build a chapel. It won't cost you a penny."

Ed Hoppes delivered to the Springfield Branch building committee a deed for two acres of land valued at about ten thousand dollars. He also offered other valuable service to assist with the building. All this because he met a young Mormon who took his religion seriously and inspired another.

— Dorothy O'Rea, "When You Least Expect It,"
Church News, January 21, 1967.

Friendship

An Unforgettable Friend

How does one become an unforgettable friend? How does one go about acquiring a large circle of friends? My friend attracted others to her as a magnet attracts steel — young and old, rich and poor, saint and sinner. What was her secret for having people regard a brief visit with her as an unforgettable occasion?

The answer is simple. She always followed her impulse to do nice things for others; she extended her friendship horizons, cultivating a new friend monthly.

She never carried hatred for anyone; she looked for people's good points and always praised their accomplishments; she was too big to dwell on hurts; she disregarded self-pity; she never condemned, but tried instead to understand. She laughed often and always bloomed where she was. Although she experienced tragedy and sorrow, losing three grown children, she was always cheerful and said, "Thy will be done."

She regarded friendship as a flower. She carefully selected the seed, kept the plant alive by the breath of good wishes, and nourished the plant until it too could bloom. She made an art of cultivating friends as one would cultivate plants.

She worked at weaving her friendship tapestry daily. Her threads consisted of the following:

When she baked bread she called all the little neighborhood boys together, then asked them to extend their hands. Their faces became radiant as she sliced and spread the bread with jam and lined up as many slices as their hands would hold.

She told pioneer stories to children that held them so spellbound they could never forget. She believed in surprises, and always gladdened children's hearts by giving little gifts — dishes, perfume, games or handkerchiefs — hidden in a dresser drawer.

Teenagers sought her advice on dating problems. Couples who had marital problems often settled their differences as she counseled them to go home and tell each other daily that they loved one another. She reminded them to keep a merry heart.

She collected rare bits of prose and poetry and humorous anecdotes, and compiled them into small plastic looseleafs which she gave to many for an anniversary, convalescence, or birthday gift.

She called the Relief Society president and asked to tend her baby while she presided over the meetings. When the president returned for her children, she handed her a casserole and a salad, saying, "You have been too busy to cook this morning. Please accept this for your lunch."

When tragedy visited a home, she took the children to her own home until the crisis was over.

She made routine telephone calls daily to cheer the lonely or discouraged, and always sent cards to remember bereavements and achievements.

She never made her trouble visible, but instead radiated sunshine with her smile.

She invited senior citizens to her home for breakfast and luncheon, and took the homebound for a ride.

She read much and was an interesting conversationalist.

She always kept in touch with relatives and expressed her love — especially to the children.

No wonder the children of the neighborhood wrote in chalk on her brick home, "We love Etta Toronto."

— Lucy G. Thomson.

I Knew You'd Come

After fighting in a bitter battle, a soldier pleaded with his commanding officer to let him go out on the battlefield to search for his missing companion. The commander said it was of no use, for no one could have lived through the hours of constant fire. The soldier insisted and was finally granted permission.

Sometime later he returned with the limp body of his dead comrade. "I told you it was useless," commented the commander.

"But you're wrong, sir. I got there in time to hear him whisper, 'I knew you'd come.'"

—Author unidentified.

Genealogy

Mrs. Wells' Dream

Brother John Wells was raised over in England; and he said that when he and his wife had sold all their furniture and were ready to leave for America, they stayed in the home of her mother. During the night (Sister Wells had had many spiritual experiences) her grandmother appeared to her and told her that when she was a young girl she heard the Mormons preach on the street. She attended one of their meetings. She was very much impressed, but her people forbade her to attend any more of the meetings. Now she said, "Since I have come here [she had passed on] the gospel has been taught to me, and I am ready for baptism. You are headed for Zion, and I would like you to do the work for me." Then she said, "You look at me and you describe me to your mother in the morning, and she'll tell you that I'm her mother." When she described this woman to her mother the next morning, her mother said, "That was my mother."

Brother Wells came over; he rented a team and buggy and drove down to Manti to do this temple work because the Salt Lake Temple was not open. These are not things that just happen. They are the things that evidence the fact that God is in this work.

— LeGrand Richards, Excerpt from a
talk given at BYU, April 4, 1972.

I'll Go Where You Want Me to Go

When I went on my first mission to Holland, three of us missionaries landed in Rotterdam, Holland, at the same time. One was from Spanish Fork, the other was from Bennington, Idaho, and I was from Salt Lake.

To make this story short, the man from Bennington, Idaho, was assigned to the northern part of Holland that we called the Groningen Conference at that time. When he received his call for his mission, his people were very much disturbed and disappointed because his ancestors were from Germany, and they wanted him to go to Germany so he could contact some of their relatives there. But the Lord inspired the President of the Church to call this boy to Holland. He inspired the mission president to assign him to that northern district. He inspired the district president to send him and his companion out to labor in the little city of Veendam, then a city of about sixty thousand. They walked along the street looking for furnished rooms and this missionary said, "This looks like a pretty good place; let's try this." They went in, rented a room, and, after they had been there a short time, found a whole record of his father's people that had been brought across the border out of Germany; and his people did not know that they had ever been in Holland.

That young man died over there of black smallpox. I took charge of his burial and his funeral because the mission president was absent from the mission and I was the secretary. The people there, the officers, after examining his effects, wanted to burn this book; and old Brother Van Braak said, "If you do it'll cost you five hundred dollars."

They said, "No book is worth five hundred dollars."

And Brother Van Braak said, "Well, that one is."

So they fumigated each page so that it could be sent home.

You could not make me believe that it was only a coincidence that this boy left Bennington, Idaho, and landed in that very house in Veendam where that record was located.

> — LeGrand Richards, Excerpt from a
> talk given at BYU, April 4, 1972.

Giving

A Father's Gift

Chance acquaintance brought the well-known writer, Leigh Mitchell Hodges, in conversation with a prosperous businessman the day before Christmas. "Would you like to know," said the businessman, "what I'm going to give my boy for Christmas?"

"Yes," replied Hodges, realizing that this father could make a very costly gift to his son. The man handed a paper to Hodges. On it was written:

"To my dear son: I give you one hour of each weekday, and two hours of my Sundays, to be yours, and to be used as you want them, without interference of any kind whatsoever. Your Father."

Hodges smiled in surprise. He wondered how that boy would feel, and what he would think, when on Christmas morning he would read that slip of paper. If he was just an average boy, he would be much dissatisfied; if he was an unusual boy, he would realize that his father had given him something he could not repay.

"Tell me," said Hodges, "how did you happen to hit upon the idea of giving such an unusual present?"

The man answered, "The other day a young fellow whom I had not seen since he was a lad about my boy's age, came to my office to 'make a touch.' His face and bearing carried the telltale marks of idleness and dissipation. He was simply a human derelict. 'Robert!' I exclaimed in amazement, 'to see you like this — and you with such a fine father!'

"The boy answered, 'Well, I've often heard that Dad was a fine man. All his friends have told me so. I never knew him. He was so much occupied with his business and his clubs that I only saw him occasionally at mealtimes. I never really knew him.'

"That made me think — and think furiously — and believe me, from now on I am going to see to it that my son has a chance to know me, be it for good or for bad."

"The greatest gift a man can give — yet a gift every father owes to his son," meditated Hodges.

— Albert Kennedy Rowswell, *Sunshine Magazine,* December 1941.

Honesty

Jim's Solution

Jim Webb lived in the high mountains of Washington. He made his living growing beautiful apples, which he wrapped and sold in many states. He gained much popularity because of the quality of the apples, and received almost more orders than he could handle.

One year Jim had an unusually large crop. But the night before he intended to pick and to bushel his crop of apples, there came a heavy rainstorm which suddenly turned into hail. All night his apples were hit by the hail. Jim had experienced severe hailstorms before and was aware of possible damage to his lovely crop. Before daylight he hastened to his orchard. Alas, the apples had been ruined!

However, Jim was a prayerful man and he humbly sought God's help. He had faith that a power greater than his could suggest something to his mind. As he arose from his knees, an idea struck him. He told his foreman and men to pick the apples and bushel them, but not put the lids on them. He then went into town and had some papers printed which read, "These apples were grown in the highest part of the northwest, and to prove this, they have hail marks on them. Because they were grown in the highest part of the northwest, the apples are more firm and retain more nectar than any other apple grown."

Today Jim Webb still receives orders for the hailstone-marked apples.

— Author unidentified.

Humility

A Lesson Learned

A young man, very confident of himself, ascended the steps to the pulpit to give his talk. Try as he would, the words failed to come. Chagrined, he bowed his head and returned to his seat. An old man sitting next to him touched his sleeve and whispered, "If you had gone up those steps as you came down, you would have come down those steps as you went up."

— Author unidentified.

Humor

You Don't Have to Go

When things get tense and serious, look for the funny side.

The story is told about one senator making a long speech. Another senator approached him and in an undertone advised him to cut his remarks short.

In a low voice, the senator who had the floor savagely told him to go to the hot place.

Later this offended senator asked President Calvin Coolidge, "Did you hear what so-and-so said to me?"

"Yes," replied Coolidge, "but I've looked up the law, and you don't have to go."

— Author unidentified.

Idleness

Ages of Service

In A.D. 109 the Romans built an aqueduct which for eighteen hundred years supplied sparkling water.

Toward the last of the nineteenth century, the Spaniards resolved to preserve the aqueduct for posterity and no longer use it for a water line. Instead they laid a modern pipeline. Soon after the flow of water ceased, the aqueduct began to fall apart. The sun's rays dried the mortar and made it crumble, the stones gave way, and soon it lay in ruins. Ages of service did not destroy this aqueduct, but idleness did.

— Author unidentified.

Inaccuracy

No Price Too High

A merchant once telegraphed to his dealer: "I have been offered fifteen thousand bushels of corn on your account at $100. Shall I buy, or is it too high a price?"

"No price too high," was the wire he received in return. What the dealer really meant was, "No, price too high." The omission of a comma changed the meaning of the message completely and cost the dealer over a thousand dollars.

He thought he was fooling the teacher when he did not learn punctuation in school.

— Author unidentified.

Kindness

Mistaken Kindness

An entomologist once amassed a comprehensive and valuable collection of moths. But one variety was lacking — an Emperor Moth — and naturally his mind was made up to be unhappy until he secured one.

By a rare stroke of good fortune one autumn he obtained a cocoon of the missing species. Then for months he hovered between joy and anxiety. Would the cocoon hatch and produce the coveted insect? He kept it in his library all winter. In the spring he examined it daily. Presently he observed signs that the moth was trying to emerge. It had succeeded in making only a tiny hole, and its struggles against the tough fiber seemed so hopeless! He resolved to ease its birth pangs. With scissors he carefully clipped the cocoon wide open. Well, the moth came out, but it never flew, and soon died. Another naturalist told him afterward that the struggles of the insect were necessary to force the strength of the body into its wings. Saving it from those struggles was a mistaken kindness.

— Author unidentified, *Sunshine Magazine,* May 1972.

Knowledge

When You Desire Knowledge

Socrates was asked by a youth how he could become a learned man. The philsopher led him to a pool of water, plunged his head under, and held it there for a few seconds.

When the surprised youth had recovered his breath, Socrates asked him, "While your head was under water, what did you desire most?"

"Air," answered the youth.

"Correct," replied Socrates. "When you desire knowledge as much as you desired air, you will find a way to get it."

— Author unidentified.

Love

Love Your Enemies

A nurse was forced by Turkish authorities to work in a military hospital. One day a patient was brought into the hospital. The nurse recognized him as the soldier who had slain her own brother, before her very eyes. She knew that the slightest inattention on her part could cause his death. Inwardly she struggled. One feeling called for vengeance, another called for love. Her better self finally conquered.

The recognition was mutual, and the wounded man asked, "Why do you not let me die?" She replied, "I am a follower of him who said, 'Love your enemies and do good to them that despitefully use you.'" Tears rolled down the face of the injured one as he said, "I never knew there was such a religion. Tell me about it."

— Author unidentified.

Marriage

We Accept Each Other

Disraeli married a wife fifteen years older than himself, and one who was not considered the brightest. His friend once expressed surprise at their happy marriage, to which Disraeli replied, "Almost daily I give thanks for my marriage. I think our success has come because we accept each other as we are. I have never tried to make Mary Anne over to my idea of how a lady should act, and she had done me the honor to let me be what God has made me. I never go home in the evening without running a little."

— Author unidentified.

Warnings of a Sick Marriage

Janie smiled ruefully and shook her head. "Maybe it's exactly what I deserve for being so smug. During the first few years I kept bragging about how *idyllic* our marriage was, always telling people how Brad and I never had a single argument; how we enjoyed each other's company and were so madly in love with each other." The smile twisted into something bitter.

"And now things have changed?" I asked. She glanced down and I saw her blue-shaded eyelids, her brows and long lashes — a beautiful, highly sensitive girl.

"It really has. Don't ask me why. There aren't any in-law problems, and we're both still faithful to each other. No money worries, no real pressures, in fact." She shrugged, and the hands in her lap turned palms up.

"The whole relationship's just sort of eroded for no logical reason — anyhow, none I can put a finger on."

"Sometimes it happens that way," I said. "No big traumatic conflict, not even any clear-cut turning point. Just a gradual erosion, as you say."

Janie's eyes were an odd mixture, a kind of sweet sadness, helplessness, hope. Eyes often convey so much more than we can ever put into words. "That's what makes it so frustrating, in a way, so sinister! If there were any real cause, even infidelity, we could at least come to grips with it."

"Oh, there are causes all right," I assured her. "Probably they're just a bit more subtle than the kind you've mentioned. They've occurred so gradually you have simply overlooked them."

"Like what?" She seemed skeptical.

"Permit me," I said, and extracted a calling card from the desk drawer. "My card." Janie examined it, then glanced at me in bewilderment. "You're looking at the wrong side," I told her. "Turn it over."

"Hmmm . . ." Her lips formed a silent whistle. "Seven Warning Signals of a Sick Marriage." "Yes," I said. "Things that often happen as people begin to take each other for granted, sometimes from sheer laziness."

The warning signals which Janie read were as follows:

1. When common courtesies are abandoned.
2. When couples begin to think in terms of "I" instead of "we."
3. When they stop complimenting each other.
4. When stubborn silence replaces common-sense communication.
5. When they stop praying together.
6. When they fail to sense and meet the needs of each other.
7. When they fail to *express* love.

Slowly Janie glanced up at me. Her face was a pool of incredulity. "You know," she said, "the only one of those warning signals we haven't experienced is number five. And that's because we never started."

I smiled. "Prayer seems rather naive to a lot of people these days, but it's always been one of my favorite prescriptions." I leaned back and stretched. It was the end of a long day.

"In any case, Janie, why not consider this little card as a personal checklist. For the next few weeks try to make a concerted, positive response on at least one or two of these items each day. Who knows? It might be contagious."

— Dr. Lindsay R. Curtis.

Mother

After Children Are Gone

A young mother writes, "I know you've written before about the empty nest. That lonely period after the children are grown and gone. Right now I'm up to my eyeballs in laundry and muddy boots. The baby is teething. The boys are fighting. My husband just called and said to eat without him and I fell off my diet. Say it to me again, will you?"

Okay, one of these days you'll shout, "Why don't you kids grow up and act your age!" And they will. Or, "You guys get outside and find yourselves something to do . . . and don't slam the door!" And they won't.

You'll prepare a perfect dinner with a salad that hasn't been picked to death and a cake with no finger traces in the icing and you'll say, "Now, there's a meal for company." And you'll eat it alone.

You'll straighten up the boys' bedroom neat and tidy . . . bumper stickers discarded . . . spread tucked and smooth . . . toys displayed on the shelves. Hangers in the closet, animals caged, and you'll say out loud, "Now I want it to stay this way," and it will.

You'll say, "I want complete privacy on the phone. No dancing around. No pantomimes. No demolition crews. Silence. Do you hear?" And you'll have it.

No more plastic tablecloths stained with spaghetti. No more bedspreads to protect the sofa from damp bottoms. No more gates to stumble over at the top of the basement steps. No more clothespins under the sofa. No more play pens to arrange a room around.

No more anxious nights under a vaporizer tent. No more sand on the sheets, or Popeye movies in the bathroom. No more iron-on patches, wet, knotted shoestrings, tight boots, or rubber bands for pony tails.

Imagine, a lipstick with a point on it. No baby sitter for New Year's Eve. Washing only once a week. Seeing a steak that isn't ground. Having your teeth cleaned without a baby on your lap. No PTA meetings. No car pools. No one washing her hair at eleven o'clock at night. Having your own roll of scotch tape.

Think about it. No more Christmas presents out of tooth-picks and library paste. No more sloppy oatmeal kisses. No more tooth fairy. No more giggles in the dark. No knees to heal, no responsibilities.

Only a voice crying, "Why don't you grow up?" And the silence echoing, "I did, Mom."

— Erma Bombeck, *Deseret News,* Copyright Field Enterprises Inc., Courtesy Publishers-Hall Syndicate.

Are There Really Angels?

"Mother," said the child, "are there really angels?"

"The Good Book says so," said the mother.

"Yes," said the child, "I have seen the picture. But did you ever see one, Mother?"

"I think I have," said the mother, "but she was not dressed like the picture."

"I am going to find one," said the child. "I am going to run along the road, miles and miles and miles, until I find an angel."

"That will be a good plan," said the mother. "And I will go with you, for you are too little to run far alone."

"I am not little any more," said the child. "I have trousers; I am big."

"So you are!" said the mother. "I forgot. But it is a fine day and I should like the walk."

"But you walk so slowly with your lame foot."

"I can walk faster than you think," said the mother.

So they started, the child leaping and running, and the mother stepping out so bravely with her lame foot that the child soon forgot about it.

The child danced on ahead, and presently he saw a carriage coming toward him drawn by prancing white horses. In the carriage sat a splendid lady in velvet and furs, with white plumes waving above her dark hair.

"Are you an angel?" asked the child, running up beside the carriage.

The lady made no reply, but stared coldly at the child; then she spoke a word to her coachman and he flicked his whip and the carriage rolled away swiftly in a cloud of dust. The dust filled the child's eyes and mouth, and made him choke and sneeze. But presently his mother came up and wiped away the dust with her blue gingham apron.

"That was not an angel!" said the child.

"No, indeed!" said the mother. "Nothing like one!"

The child danced on again, leaping and running from side to side of the road, and the mother followed as best she might.

By and by the child met a most beautiful maiden, clad in a white dress. Her eyes were like blue stars and her cheeks like roses.

"I am sure you must be an angel!" cried the child.

"You dear little child!" cried the maiden. "Someone else said that once. Do I really look like an angel?"

"You are an angel!" said the child.

The maiden took him up in her arms and kissed him, and held him tenderly.

"You are the dearest little thing I ever saw," she said. "Tell me, what makes you think so?"

But suddenly her face changed.

"Someone is coming to meet me!" she cried, "and you have soiled my white dress with your dusty shoes, and pulled my hair all down. Run away, child, and go home to your mother!" She sat the child down so hastily that he stumbled and fell; but she did not see that, for she was hastening forward to meet her friend.

The child lay in the dusty road and sobbed, till his mother came along and picked him up and wiped away the tears with her blue gingham apron.

"I don't believe that was an angel, after all," he said.

"No," said the mother, "but she may be one someday. She is young yet."

"I am tired," said the child. "Will you carry me home, Mother?"

"Why yes," said the mother, "that is what I came for."

The child put his arms around his mother's neck, and she held him tight and trudged along the road singing the song he liked best.

Suddenly he looked up in her face.

"Mother," he said, "I know you are an angel!"

"Oh, what a foolish child!" said the mother. "Who ever heard of an angel in a blue gingham apron?" And she went on singing and stepped out so bravely on her lame foot that no one would ever have known she was lame.

But we know the boy had found his angel.

— *Deseret News.*

She Was a Mother
(A True Story)

The dreaded outlaw Pancho Villa was coming soon from his mountain stronghold to attack Cruces. Consternation reigned in that doomed village, for only too well her people knew what to expect when that ruthless horde of bandits swooped down on a village hot with lust for its fiery liquors, its precious loot, and its lovely maidens.

Knowing their inability to defend their homes, the citizens hastily loaded their most precious belongings into wagons and ox carts, or packed them on the backs of their slow-moving but dependable burros, and headed for their stronghold a few miles distant in the gorges of the Sierras.

They had made this same move many times during the revolutions of past years, so that now even the beasts of burden seemed instinctively to sense their destination. Hurriedly, yet in good order, they made their way to safety, leaving a small company of expert riflemen to observe and harass their enemies should they show any disposition to pursue the fugitives.

As was usually the case, Villa's attack on the village was made just before the dawn of day and great was the surprise of the marauders when they dashed up the silent streets clear to the Plaza without sighting a single person or receiving any reply to the volleys of bullets fired through the windows and doors of the houses as they passed.

Villa and his men were furious as they began to realize that their prey had flown. They had left behind them, it was true, a much appreciated supply of corn, chile and frijoles, but none of the really precious supply of arms, ammunition or pesos they had hoped to secure as a reward for their efforts. Hard, indeed, would be the lot of the traitor who had betrayed the plans of his chief, could they but lay hands upon him.

And catch him they did that very day, for the promise of a reward proved too much for the loyalty of a supposed friend and that night Julian Medina lay in fetters with the sentence of death upon him, to be carried out at daybreak. Knowing as he did the implacable hatred his chief had for those who betrayed his trust, the prisoner had no hope of any leniency. The shadow of his impending doom shut out the sunlight of hope.

But how could he have done other than he did — he in whose veins ran the blood of old Castile mingled with the no less proud strain of the Aztec emperors? For not only was his gray-haired *mamacita* living there, but it was also the home of the maiden whom he some day hoped to make his bride. And what allegiance could he owe to that ruthless chief who had forced him against his will into the ranks of his marauders, and who would inflict upon him death for desertion should he be caught out of the ranks without leave of absence. Surely now his doom was sealed, but death would be sweetened by the knowledge that his own life was but paying the price of safety for his loved ones.

And so the hours dragged their weary way along and the last dawn his eyes would ever see was not far away. His dismal meditations were interrupted by the opening of the door and in came his old friend and confessor, Padre Leon, who had now come to prepare him to leave this world. This same good man had christened him and had always been his staunch amigo.

Scarcely had the door closed, however, when the amazed Julian found himself being covered with kisses by the supposed priest, whose hood now fell back and disclosed the tear-stained face of his own little mother, who had thus, with the connivance of Padre Leon, braved death in the hope of saving her son. They would change clothes and he would go out to liberty as a priest, while she would remain as the prisoner to meet whatever fate might await her. Against this plan Julian set his face with fierce determination, but what chance had his will against that of a mother who was determined that, come what might to her, Julian must be set free.

To make the necessary change of apparel was but the work of a moment and soon the supposed Padre had passed the sleepy guards who were still feeling the effects of the liquor they had drunk the previous day. As the good Padre was used to coming and going at will through the camp, little attention was paid to him and soon the fugitive was beyond the reach of his enemies.

Great was the wrath of Don Pancho when he learned of his prisoner's escape and furious were his threats of vengeance upon the traitor who had given him his liberty. But when the culprit was ushered into his presence and he discovered who it was that tricked him, his thirst for vengeance underwent a change.

To his question as to why she dared to thwart his plans, the little mother reminded him that he himself had once had a mother who would willingly have dared as much for him and, after all, it was not the part of a great man to make war upon women. Whether it was memories of a long-forgotten childhood that softened his heart or just some lingering strain of chivalry towards womankind that brought the change matters not.

Senora Medina was furnished with a horse and an escort to return to her people, who hailed her as one risen from the dead.

— Theodore Martineau.

Parents

That Not One Child Be Lost

Seven-year-old Tommy had just finished his breakfast and started out to play. His mother called after him, "Don't go to Danny's, Tommy. Play in our yard this morning." Tommy paid no attention. He continued going — straight toward Danny's. His mother stepped outside and called, "Well if you must go, at least wait for your little brother and take him with you."

As Tommy's mother returned to her household chores, she gave the incident no further thought. She would have been amazed if someone had told her that she was seriously endangering her son's future by failing to teach him to obey her. And yet Tommy's safety may be threatened many times if he is not willing to obey those who care about his welfare. If he does not learn to respect authority, he will be handicapped in his later life when he tries to fit into a society that must be governed by law. Even his eternal destiny is at stake, because if he does not learn to obey his earthly parents, he may also fail to obey his Heavenly Father.

Tommy's mother loves him and yet she had failed to realize that teaching him to obey is an important part of loving him. She could profit from the words of an older mother whose son is in prison, who said, "I am more to blame than my boy. I thought I was being kind to him when I let him do as he pleased, but I know now that I failed him. Society is trying to teach him to respect authority — something he should have learned from me when he was a child." Parents show true love for their children when they take the time and make the effort necessary to teach them to obey.

— Erma Y. Gardiner, *Children's Friend,* April 1961.

Before It Is Too Late

"What color are kites?" Four-year-old Becky called the question to her mother, Mary, who was coming up the basement steps, carrying a basket of wet clothes.

"Oh, kites are just any color," answered her mother as she glanced at the kitchen clock through the open doorway.

"But what color?" persisted Becky. "I want to make this page in my coloring book look pretty." Her mother never heard. She had already hurried out the back door, her mind completely centered on the fact that if she hurried, she could get her clothes hung before 10:00 A.M.

As she stepped into the brisk wind, Mary heard the happy shouts of children. Looking toward the sound, she saw her neighbor Millie holding on to the string of a kite. Her two pre-school children were shouting with glee as they watched the kite soar in the breezes.

"Why, Millie," called Mary, "how do you ever find time to fly kites? I never get through, with just two children. And you have five!"

Millie handed the kite string to Bobby and came toward

Mary. "Of course I don't really have time," she laughed, "but I take time. And that is just as much fun. I knew my laundry would wait. As Bobby said, the wind was just right and it might stop."

"Well, you are different than I," said Mary, with a gesture of impatience, "I like to get my work done."

"Yes, I know," said Millie. "I used to feel that way, too, but a toy horse made me change." Mary looked puzzled, so Millie continued. "When my oldest boy was three years old, he saw a stuffed toy horse that belonged to my sister's little boy. He fell in love with that horse. It was all he wanted for his birthday, so I borrowed the pattern. But time slipped by and I never got it made. After his birthday, he went on wanting it. He asked Santa to bring it. I bought some cloth and cut it out, but I was busy, so it wasn't finished by Christmas. He was so disappointed, I made up my mind to finish it right away, but it was several months later when I finally presented it to him. He wasn't excited. He only said, 'It's pretty. Let's give it to baby brother.' He had changed. It was too late to give him a toy horse. In a flash of panic I thought of the stories he had wanted, the questions he had asked. It was too late for them, too. It might even get too late to teach him the things I wanted him to know about the gospel. The thought frightened me. As I said, I changed. I take time for the children now, even if it means hurrying through my work."

Just then Bobby shouted, "Come right now, Mother. The kite is falling down!" Millie hurried away and Mary turned to the clothes basket. As she glanced at the kite, she thought, "That kite is red and blue. I'll have to tell Becky when I go in." Then a thought struck her. When she got back in the house, it would probably be too late; Becky would have the kites all colored. *Too late!* Mary dropped the clothes back into the basket. All at once it seemed more important to talk to Becky about kites than to hang up the clothes.

— Erma Y. Gardiner, *Children's Friend,* July 1961.

Praise

The Music of the Bells

On a pedestal in one of the famous old churches of
Europe is a statue of a nobleman with a string of bells about
his waist. The church was erected centuries before America
was discovered, and among the many legends woven into its
history, one of the most interesting is the one of the nobleman's
statue.

An orphaned brother and sister, the only surviving mem-
bers of a noble and very wealthy family, owned an immense
section of the country and ruled the lives of the peasants of
that territory.

The sister was a beautiful character, amiable, charming,
and loved by all. The brother was a veritable autocrat, domi-
neering and egotistical. Whenever anyone antagonized him,
he would fly into a violent rage, and if any unfortunate serf
dared to disobey him, or interfere with his pleasure, he would
strike him down.

The sister, chagrined at her brother's conduct, sought to
cure him of his annoying weakness. Without telling him of
her purpose, she suggested that together they build a great
church. But each was to erect half of the church independent
of the other.

The vanity of the undertaking appealed to the brother,
and construction was started. In time the brother discovered
that his sister was making faster progress. The sister told him
that this was because he was always quarreling with his workmen, keeping them from doing their best. The sister asked him
to let her tie a string of bells about him. The bells, she said,
would help to hasten the building because, as he approached
the men, they would hear the jingling and hasten to work,
thus saving much time otherwise lost.

The brother thought it a novel idea. When he heard the jingle of the bells it was like sweet music in his ears, and it soothed his temper. And when he approached the men, he found everyone busily at work. This also pleased him. Finding them diligent, he praised and encouraged them, and they did better work. Before many days he was actually popular with his men.

Spurred by a newborn spirit of pride in their work, the men began to vie with their fellows on the sister's side of the church, and finally finished their half first, to the joy of both brother and sister.

One day, long after the church was finished, the sister revealed to her brother the innocent deception she had played on him to cure him of his evil disposition. The nobleman was so impressed with the lesson he had learned that he had a statue of himself with the bells made, to remind him, and others like him, of the power of goodwill, praise, and encouragement in dealing with others.

— Author unidentified.

Prayer

Can You Teach Johnny to Pray?

Ellen Blair sat motionless. Aimlessly her eyes followed the delicate patterns on the wall made by the first rays of the morning sun as it filtered through the glass doors on the hospital corridor. The sparrows in the cypress tree outside the window had begun their twittering, and she realized the long night's vigil had passed.

A deep ache filled her heart. She was grateful to have her husband, Michael, beside her. It was he who had answered the telephone call last night that had summoned them to

Valley Hospital. The brief explanation was that there had been an automobile accident following the commencement exercises at the high school. Their son Robert, still in his cap and gown, had been seriously injured.

Ellen blinked as if to blot out the image of the still, white face of her oldest son, lying unconscious on the elevated pillows in the emergency room.

"Concussion, skull fracture," the doctor had said. "The spinal tap showed blood in it, so we must do a craniotomy right away to try to locate the bleeding. If we stop the hemorrhage, there is a chance; if not —" But he had not continued.

They had sat in the waiting room through the long hours, each praying silently. Ellen trembled as the realization of her son's serious condition again enveloped her.

Suddenly an unexpected commotion broke the quiet of the early dawn. It was Johnny Hansen, Robert's closest friend, who dashed through the swinging door. His tousled brown hair showed a quick combing. His white shirt, not completely tucked in, gave evidence of his rush.

"I just heard about Bob! How bad —"

Seeing the anxiety in the faces before him, he did not finish his question. Ellen tried to explain the seriousness of Robert's injuries, but her voice broke and she gave way to quiet crying. Michael carried on.

As their whispering voices became a monotone, Ellen's thoughts drifted back over the years since that August day eighteen years ago, when Robert was born in this same hospital. . . .

He had been such a red-faced little mite, as scrawny as a baby bird. How quickly the time had passed! It seemed only yesterday that he was fumbling and struggling over his new tricycle, still tied with Christmas ribbons. Before there had been time to think about it, Robert had gone to his first day of school, a little frightened, perhaps, but quite grown up in new blue jeans and red corduroy shirt. How many times she had wanted to fix these pictures forever in her mind! But each new stage replaced the last, and Robert showed an eagerness for all sorts of activity. Primary classes provided new growth, and the Cub pack brought wider fields to explore.

About this time the Hansens moved next door. In a neighborly way she sent Robert over with a plate of cookies, and in return he brought Johnny home with him.

It was not until a few days passed that she realized how much Johnny's environment was unlike Robert's. The ideals and standards were quite the reverse in Johnny's home. Drinking, smoking, and foul language were commonplace, and religion played no part at all in their way of life. She was reluctant to have Robert cultivate this friendship, but the two boys seemed drawn together like magnets.

Since Johnny was three years older than Robert, he was more mature and became an ideal in the eyes of her eight-year-old. They were always together. Then, in a child's most natural way, Johnny began to go to Primary with Robert.

One day the two boys came racing home from Primary, Johnny in the lead until they reached the door. Then he shyly stood behind it while Robert anxiously grasped her hand, pulled her into the hallway, and whispered into her ear.

"Mom, can you teach Johnny to pray?"

The unexpected request brought a lump to her throat when she looked at this shy, sensitive boy who normally bluffed his way with a rough exterior. He had been asked to give the opening prayer in Primary the next Wednesday.

"Of course we will help Johnny."

She went into the living room, and the boys followed her.

"You know what prayer really is, don't you, Johnny?"

"Yeah, I guess so."

"Jesus said that whatever righteous desire we ask for in prayer, if we believe, we will receive it."

"He did?"

"Yes. Prayer is not only words; it is talking with our Heavenly Father. Have you heard the hymn we sing at church that says, 'Prayer is the soul's sincere desire'?" She hummed a few strains of the hymn.

"Yeah."

"You know, Mom, they sang it at Primary conference," Robert commented, wanting to help with this important project.

"There are certain words we use in praying to show reverence and respect, such as thee and thou, and thy and thine. One of the first things we express in prayer is our thankfulness for our many blessings. You know what your blessings are, I'm sure."

"I guess everything good is a blessing," Johnny answered.

Together they wrote out a very brief outline for a prayer, and Johnny agreed to work on it.

The following Wednesday when Robert came home from Primary, he was not his usual exuberant self, and the absence of Johnny was noticeable. Ellen could not help asking, "Robert, how did Johnny get along with the opening prayer?" But Robert evaded the question. With a shrug he went to his room.

Although perturbed, Ellen did not pursue the subject, but she asked Sister Lindley, the Primary president, about it when she met her the next day at the market.

"Oh, he tried," she said, "but he was so frightened after muttering a few inaudible words, he turned and ran out the door."

Her thoughts drifted next to the summer evening when Johnny was at their home at dinner. She and Michael gathered their children around the dinner table to kneel for family prayer. Since Johnny appeared reluctant to leave, she asked, "Would you like to join us?"

Johnny nodded and had just fallen to his knees beside Robert when Mr. Hansen's bellowing voice came through the open window. "Johnny! Johnny! Where is that good-for-nothing kid? He better get home or —"

She saw the red creep up the boy's neck as he murmured, "I gotta go."

Obviously dreading the encounter with his father, he slipped out the back door.

The summer Robert was ordained to the priesthood, Johnny asked if he might be baptized. The bond between the boys seemed stronger than ever and soon Johnny was also ordained a deacon. She remembered when he asked her husband, Michael, to explain a quotation he had heard in his quorum meeting: ". . . no man taketh this honour unto himself, but he that is called of God, as was Aaron."

"Even Jesus Christ himself had to be called of God, Johnny. He left the priesthood on the earth with his apostles, and they used it until there was a great apostasy of Christ's Church," Michael had patiently explained.

"Then how come we have it now?" asked Johnny.

"You know the story of Joseph Smith?"

"Sure."

"Well, in 1829 the priesthood was restored to Joseph by a heavenly messenger," Michael had continued.

"You mean it was passed down to us from the Prophet?"

"From the Prophet Joseph Smith or Oliver Cowdery — they both received it at the same time."

Michael had felt some reservation about the young boy's comprehension of the priesthood and its true purpose, but he appreciated the boy's concern for it.

Soon after Johnny had been ordained a priest, he was asked to administer the sacrament in Sunday School. When he refused, his priests quorum adviser told him it was very simple: the card with the prayer written on it would be on the sacrament table, and he could read it, so he finally reluctantly agreed.

The first young priest blessed the bread. Then it was Johnny's turn to bless the water. He began falteringly, then stopped. He had misread the words. Again he started, and again he misread the words. The bishop asked him to repeat it, and a third time he started, then faltered and stopped. There was a tenseness in the air that could be felt throughout the congregation. Then suddenly Johnny stood up, crimson-faced, and left the chapel, while the other priest quietly took his place and gave the blessing on the water. It was many weeks before Johnny came back to church.

The Blairs had wondered what changes would take place when Johnny was graduated from high school. Would the friendship that had developed between these two boys fade? But college life did not spoil the admiration Johnny held for his young friend, and it was during the first semester of his second year that he had written Robert of his thrill at meeting the girl he planned to marry. He had added, "She is a wonderful girl, Bob, and a member of the Church. We wonder if your parents would go with us when we are married in the temple."

Ellen and Michael did accompany Johnny and his young bride to the temple. And as she saw them kneeling at the altar, she heard again in her mind Robert's childish plea, "Mom, can you teach Johnny to pray?"

Ellen was snapped abruptly back to reality as the white stretcher was wheeled down the hall. Terrible fear gripped her again as she looked at Robert's still form, his head swathed in bandages. Helplessly she looked at Michael, then at Johnny. A tear was trickling down his cheek.

The stretcher was wheeled into a room and the door closed behind it. When it opened again the two men in white wheeled the empty stretcher out, and a nurse came to the door.

"Dr. Klein, the specialist, is still in surgery, but he'll be here soon to talk with you. Dr. Snow is coming now," she said, nodding toward the doctor coming down the hall.

Both the doctor and nurse stepped into the room and again closed the door, leaving Michael, Ellen, and Johnny waiting in the hall.

Time seemed to stand still; then Dr. Snow reappeared and indicated that they should come in. His deep voice, though hardly above a whisper, seemed like the roar of a lion when he said, "Your son is not responding. I will call Dr. Klein, but I'm afraid it might be too late."

"Why? Oh, why?" Ellen sobbed.

It was Johnny's voice she heard now, faltering, "Please, could I pray for him?"

Not knowing exactly what to do, Johnny knelt clumsily beside the bed. The words came from the very depth of his soul, direct and meaningful, in gratitude for all that Robert had meant to him and for the teachings that had found a place, bit by bit, in his life. With firm conviction, he pleaded for the life of his friend. ". . . but in all things, Father in heaven," he prayed, "even in this, we ask that thy will, not ours, be done, but give us the wisdom to understand. . . ."

The door opened. It was Dr. Klein, still in his surgical gown. "Dr. Snow just talked to me. We have done all we can do. I'm sorry," Dr. Klein said softly.

From years of habit the doctor automatically placed his fingers on his patient's wrist. He hesitated, then hastily but gently pulled back the sheet and placed his stethoscope on the boy's chest. Several times he shifted the stethoscope. He looked puzzled, and the furrows deepened between his shaggy brows.

For many seconds no word was spoken. Then he abruptly ordered the nurse, "Replace the oxygen tent."

Ellen heard in her mind once more, "Mom, can you teach Johnny to pray?"

— Jane Jamison, *Improvement Era*, June 1968.

He Has a Spiritual Wealth
(J. C. Penney's Own Story)

From my vantage point of nearly 99 years, I have reached one Gibraltar-sure conclusion about life: We cannot perform the high tasks of life without the help of God. We cannot do our duty without faith in him. We cannot succeed without constant prayer.

My own long life has taught me this painfully, yet perfectly. Trained by my parents to live by the Golden Rule, I long thought of myself as a religious man. I had confidence in God's goodness, especially as the Penney stores grew in numbers and profits.

Like so many of my fellowmen, I thought it was sufficient to do the right thing, to be self-reliant, hard-working, ambitious. But, in time, I learned one can be too self-reliant.

Through all the years I was building my business, I worked out many intricate financial transactions, supervised merchandise purchasing, production, and distribution, dealt with thousands of men inside and outside the Penney company.

In all these matters, my basic feeling was that everything was up to me; I had to make all the right decisions myself. And, of course, as my sense of power increased, I felt that with more and more money I could move mountains.

I was still, I believe, a religious man, but more and more the spiritual side of my thinking and living filled a separate compartment. I still governed myself by the Golden Rule, but I confess it freely, God had very little hand in my life and business.

Then came the tidal wave we called the Depression — the black years from 1929 to 1932 which engulfed individuals in every corner of the country. My interests were far flung — the Christian Herald Association, the Penney Retirement Community, the National Youth Radio Conference were three major endeavors among many others. In order to finance these and other projects, I had borrowed heavily from several banks. Then, when the stock market collapsed, several of the banks demanded that I repay them, which I was unable to do; as a result, they foreclosed on the heavy collateral I had put up. In an effort to sustain these projects during this period, I poured even more money into them, resulting in my debts exceeding seven million dollars. In the end, I lost almost my entire personal estate, which I valued at forty million dollars. This was a most bitter, soul-searing experience of my life; but I learned some valuable lessons, principally that money won't insure success.

In this crisis of my life, I had many inner obstacles to overcome. Constantly in those days I carried a slip of paper on which I'd written (from Psalm 91) : "He shall cover thee with his feathers, and under his wings shall thou trust. His truth shall be thy shield and buckler."

It took much time, as well as an entirely new kind of personal discipline, to clarify my thinking more about the power of God and less about the power of money.

I found myself not only nearly broke at fifty-six but discouraged and ill in a sanatorium in Battle Creek, Michigan. I felt that I would never see the dawn of another day. I got up and wrote farewell letters to my wife and to my oldest son. I sealed the letters. If I did sleep, it was not a sound sleep. I rose early, went down to the mezzanine floor, and found the dining room was not open.

As I proceeded down the corridor, I heard voices coming from a distance, singing gospel hymns. I followed the singing and came to a chapel in the sanatorium and went in. The hymn being sung as I entered was an old favorite, "God Will Take Care of You." You can imagine my heavy heart when I walked in; but I came out lifted of this burden and a changed man. Within just a few moments my life was transformed. It was almost as if I had had a new birth. God did take care of me. He did save me. And ever since, I have been trying to fill that obligation.

When I finally got back on firm ground, I had much less in a material sense than I enjoyed before. But I had gained immeasurably in spiritual wealth, for I had learned to turn to God for guidance in all the acts and decisions of my life.

All spiritual awakening requires this realization: material arrogance and pride build up a sense of power that separates man more and more from God. Then when some desperate crisis brings this realization, the change appears almost a miracle.

But that miracle is ever within a hand's reach of all of us. That is the wonderful thing about it. We have only to reach out and touch God, to take his hand and ask him to lead us.

— Deseret News.

Revelation

An Incident Connected with the Building of the Salt Lake Temple

Work proceeded on the substructure until it had reached a height of about two feet above the surface of the ground. Then cracks in it were discovered and other defects were noted. After serious consideration, President Young and his advisors decided that the foundation would not sustain the tremendous weight to be placed upon it. What should be done? President Young dismissed the workmen, and sitting down on the foundation said, "Here I shall remain until the Lord reveals to me what I should do next."

He had not been there long when my father came into view. President Young motioned him to come to him. "Bishop, sit down," he said, and then told him of his problem.

They went carefully over the matter in hand, the foundation, the material, the manner in which it had been put together. Then President Young said, "Bishop, can you tell me what to do?"

"Yes, the trouble is the use of too much mortar. The settling has caused the walls to crack. You must tear out the entire foundation and start over again. This time have the stones in the entire building cut to fit exactly and placed stone upon stone with precise fittings. This will prevent cracking, settling, or spreading in any way."

President Young brought his hand down on Father's shoulder, "You are right. That is my revelation."

The workmen returned. The entire foundation was torn out and the walls rebuilt according to Father's instructions. Very little if any mortar was used.

Why did this revelation come through Father? Because his life had been spent working out practical problems and so he was equal to the occasion.

> — From the biography of Archibald Gardner, as recorded by his son, Clarence Gardner, *Children's Friend.*

Service

Goodness in Each

The following story illustrates the innate goodness in each one of us.

A young mother boarded a train with many others. No one helped her with her babies and parcels. The conductor put his arm across the entrance and asked if anyone would please help the lady. Immediately one picked up the baby, another the baggage, and soon the lady was situated.

All were willing to assist, but someone had to call good out.

— Author unidentified.

Tolerance

A Different Point of View

Two bricklayers began an argument over their work which soon developed into a real quarrel. Angry words were followed by blows. In a few moments they were engaged in a savage fight. Overseers hurried to the scene and endeavored to pull the two men apart. When they were quieted down sufficiently to give an explanation, this was the cause of their quarrel: One man said the mortar in a brick was to hold it apart; the other one said it was to keep it together.

— Author unidentified.

Trouble

Philosophy

"The camel's nose is under the tent" is an expression that comes from an old Arabian fable, and to an Arab it spells trouble. This is the story:

One cold night, a camel thrust his nose under a flap of an Arab's tent and looked in.

"It is cold and stormy without; please let me put my nose under your tent."

"You are welcome," said the Arab, and turned over and went to sleep.

A little later he awoke and found the camel had not only put his nose in the tent, but his neck and head as well. The camel, who kept twisting his head from right to left, said, "Could I not put my forelegs within the tent? It will take but a little more room and it is so awkward for me to stand half in and half out." The Arab moved a little to make room as he consented to let the camel put in his forelegs.

Finally, the camel said, "I keep the tent open by standing as I do, may I not come wholly inside?"

"Perhaps it will be better for us both," said the Arab. "Do come in." So the camel crowded into the tent.

The next time the Arab awoke he was outside the tent in the cold, and the camel had the tent to himself.

-— Author unidentified.

Work

Something Earned

An aging father had a business that he knew would eventually go to his son. The father desired to take things easier, so he announced that if his son could bring him five hundred dollars that he had earned himself (something the son had never done before), the business would be his from that moment on.

The mother of the boy decided to help her son (as she had always done). Quietly she gave him five hundred dollars and told him to dress in the clothes of a laborer when he brought the money of his father.

"Here, Father, is the five hundred dollars that I have made myself," said the boy.

The father took the money and, without looking up from his evening paper, tossed the money into the fireplace where it was consumed by the fire.

"Son," said the mother later, "You weren't convincing — and you've got to be convincing around your father. Now here's another five hundred dollars. Try it again."

This time the son made sure that he had dirtied his clothes and his hands and then appeared physically tired when he came to his father with the money.

The father did the same as before. Without looking up from his paper, he threw the five hundred dollars on the fire while the son watched horrified.

With this turn of events, the son decided that perhaps he had better go out and really make the five hundred dollars. His father, he realized, would be convinced in no other way. At long last he came to his father with another five hundred dollars.

But again the father, without looking up, threw the money into the fireplace.

Instantly the son reached into the flames and pulled back the money.

"Son," the father said, looking up from the paper, "I see that you've earned *that* money."

— Author unidentified.